05

FULLMETAL EDITION

FULLMETAL ALCHEMIST

by HIROMU ARAKAWA

05

FULLMETAL EDITION

FULLMETAL ALCHEMIST

by HIROMU ARAKAWA

FULLMETAL EDITION

FULLMETAL ALCHEMIST

05
CONTENTS

FOO

OM

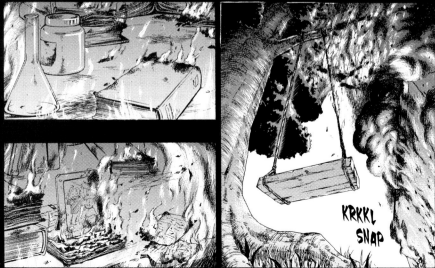

KRKKL
SNAP

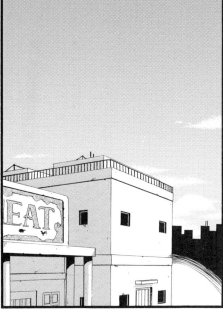

...A COFFIN STORE! GO AND BUY TWO IN YOUR SIZES!!

KRIK KRIK KRIK

EEP——!!

DOWN THE ROAD ABOUT THREE BLOCKS YOU'LL FIND...

Sigh...

I TOLD YOU TIME AND TIME AGAIN TO STAY AWAY FROM HUMAN TRANSMUTATION.

Sigh!

ALL JOKES ASIDE...

WAIT, TEACHER, YOU ALSO...?

SO THE STUDENT MAKES THE SAME MISTAKE AS THE TEACHER.

YOU GUYS REALLY ARE THE BIGGEST FOOLS.

...SOME OF MY INSIDES.

THEY TOOK...

WE'RE SORRY.

RUNT!!

Y-YES, MA'AM...

NUMB-SKULLS!

YOU'RE RIGHT.

FOOLS!

YES, MA'AM.

WE'RE SO SORRY.

MORONS!

IT MUST HAVE BEEN TOUGH.

...SO I GUESS WE KIND OF GOT WHAT WE DESERVED.

NO. WE BROUGHT IT ON OUR-SELVES...

YOU FOOLS.

UH-HUH.

RIGHT?

YOU DON'T HAVE TO HOLD BACK.

NO WAY!

MOST PEOPLE WOULD CALL THAT *GENIUS.*

IF YOU CAME BACK ALIVE AFTER SEEING *THAT THING,* THEN THAT'S MORE THAN ENOUGH PROOF TO CALL YOU A GENIUS.

IT'S JUST THAT I SAW *THAT THING.*

I'M NO GENIUS.

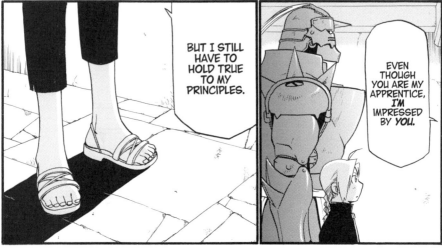

BUT I STILL HAVE TO HOLD TRUE TO MY PRINCIPLES.

EVEN THOUGH YOU ARE MY APPRENTICE, *I'M* IMPRESSED BY *YOU.*

YOU'RE BOTH EXPELLED.

AL.

BUT, TEACHER...

YOU'RE NO LONGER MY APPRENTICES.

I DIDN'T TEACH YOU ALCHEMY SO THAT YOU COULD END UP WITH BODIES LIKE THOSE.

WHILE SHE WAS PREGNANT WITH HER FIRST CHILD, IZUMI BECAME DEATHLY ILL.

SHE SAID "I'M SORRY" THE WHOLE NIGHT LONG...

...AND IT WASN'T EVEN HER FAULT.

AFTER THAT SHE WAS LEFT WITH A BODY THAT COULD NEVER GIVE BIRTH AGAIN.

SHE FOUGHT HARD AND THE DOCTORS DID THEIR BEST, BUT THE CHILD DIDN'T MAKE IT TO TERM.

BUT I WAS THE FOOL FOR NOT REALIZING WHAT SHE WAS UP TO SOONER.

AND YOU ALREADY KNOW THE RESULT.

I THINK THAT'S WHEN SHE STARTED THINKING ABOUT HUMAN TRANS-MUTATION.

COME ON BY IF YOU'RE EVER IN THE AREA.

HUH ?

BUT...

STATION

DON'T YOU GET IT? NOW THAT YOU NO LONGER HAVE A MASTER–APPRENTICE RELATIONSHIP...

ARE YOU REALLY THAT DUMB?!

YEAH.

WE'VE BEEN EXPELLED, SO...

SO DO YOU STILL THINK THERE'S ANY NEED TO STAY AWAY?

HM?

...IT MEANS YOU CAN SPEAK TO ONE ANOTHER AS PEERS.

SCRUFF
SCRUFF

AWWWWW...

DAMMIT!!

DASH

GOOD.

THANKS, MR. CURTIS! WE'RE GOING BACK!

AL! WHAT DID WE COME TO DUBLITH FOR, ANYWAY?!

OH!!

TM TM TM TM TM

TM TM

WE'LL TRY OUR BEST!

STATION

DON'T LET HER KILL YOU!

WE'RE NOT LEAVING!

LEAVE!

NO!!

I TOLD YOU TO LEAVE. NOW GET THE HELL OUT!!

WE'RE NOT LEAVING, EVEN IF YOU CUT US UP!!

I'LL CUT YOU!!

20

YOU IDIOTS.

THEY HAVE THE SAME EYES AS BACK THEN...

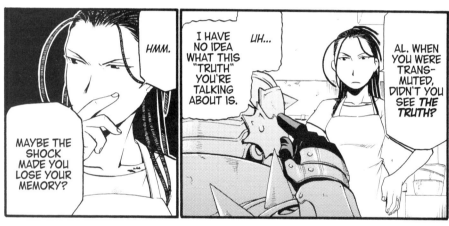

HMM.

MAYBE THE SHOCK MADE YOU LOSE YOUR MEMORY?

I HAVE NO IDEA WHAT THIS "TRUTH" YOU'RE TALKING ABOUT IS.

UH...

AL. WHEN YOU WERE TRANS-MUTED, DIDN'T YOU SEE *THE TRUTH*?

THAT GUY TALKED ABOUT PAYING THE *TOLL*! I JUST PAID MY ARM AND MY LEG...BUT WITH WHAT AL PAID, HE MUST HAVE BEEN CLOSEST TO THE *TRUTH*!

I GET IT!

WE HAVE TO GET AL'S MEMORY BACK.

AFTER ALL, HIS ENTIRE BODY WAS TAKEN. THINK WHAT HE MIGHT HAVE EXPERIENCED.

HUH? WHAT THING? IS IT THAT BAD?

YEAH, *THAT THING.*

BUT THE MEMORY OF *THAT THING...*

SO IF I CAN REMEMBER WHAT HAPPENED, WE'LL HAVE THE ANSWER?!

THAT'S TOO ABSTRACT. I DON'T GET IT!

YEAH.

REALLY WEIRD.

Kinda looks like this?

MORE LIKE WEIRD.

IT'S NOT BAD, PER SE.

Like this.

BUT STILL...

IT COULD LEAVE HIM A VEGETABLE, HUH?

ER...

HE MIGHT LOSE HIS MIND.

IF THERE'S A CHANCE IT MIGHT HELP, I *WANT TO TRY IT!*

OKAY.

I'LL TRY TO FIND A WAY TO RETRIEVE YOUR MEMORY.

I'M GOING TO ASK AN ACQUAINTANCE OF MINE ABOUT THIS.

BUT BEFORE I DO THAT...

ARE YOU GONNA SIT THERE ALL NIGHT? MOVE!

Y-YES, MA'AM!!

THANK YOU VERY MUCH!!

...YOU MUST BE HUNGRY.

I'LL MAKE SOME DINNER.

GIVE ME A HAND.

YOU'RE NOT LEAVING UNTIL YOU FIND YOUR ANSWERS, RIGHT?

COMMANDING GENERAL

YOUR TRANSFER ORDER HAS ARRIVED.

YES, SIR.

YOU'LL BE WORKING IN CENTRAL, STARTING NEXT WEEK.

NO, I'M NOT HALF AS INTERESTING AS THE STORIES OF YOU IN YOUR PRIME.

TAP

YOU BROUGHT A LITTLE COLOR TO THIS DREARY DESERT.

IT WON'T BE THE SAME WITHOUT YOU.

25

26

...IF YOU REALLY WANT TO HELP ME OUT, THERE ARE SOME SUBORDINATES THAT I WOULD LIKE TO TAKE WITH ME TO CENTRAL.

BUT, YOU KNOW...

THANK YOU, SIR. I OWE YOU.

YES, OF COURSE.

TAKE ANYONE YOU'D LIKE.

HEY!

CHECK-MATE!

BAM

IT JUST GOES TO SHOW THAT YOU CAN'T JUDGE A PERSON BY HIS APPEARANCE.

YOU MEAN HE'S NOT JUST A MEATHEAD?

DAMMIT!!

MWA HA HA HA! FIFTEEN CONSECUTIVE WINS!

HEY, WHAT'S ALL THE COMMOTION?

The forehead?

HEH HEH HEH. A SOLDIER SHOULD BE ALL ABOUT *THIS*, UP *HERE!*

...BUT IT'S FROM SOME ISLAND COUNTRY IN THE EAST.

IT'S CALLED "SHOGI." IT'S LIKE CHESS...

OH. THAT'S AN UNUSUAL GAME YOU HAVE THERE.

OH, I ALMOST FORGOT! I CAME HERE ON AN ERRAND.

ALL RIGHT, NEXT. WHO'S NEXT?

SHOGI: [PRONOUNCED SHOW-GEE] A TWO-PLAYER STRATEGY GAME PLAYED ON A BOARD OF 81 SQUARES WITH 20 PIECES PER SIDE. PLAYERS TAKE TURNS MOVING ONE PIECE ACCORDING TO ITS FUNCTION AND ATTEMPT TO TAKE THE OPPONENT'S KING. ITS ORIGINS ARE—

YES, I KNOW.

ME? AND YOU?

HE ASKED ME TO GO WITH YOU AS WELL.

THE COLONEL WANTS TO SEE YOU.

YES.

HOW'S THAT?

THAT SHOULD DO IT.

Phew.

Thank you, sir!

THANK YOU, MASTER SERGEANT FUERY!

OH! IT'S CONNECTED.

TELEPHON

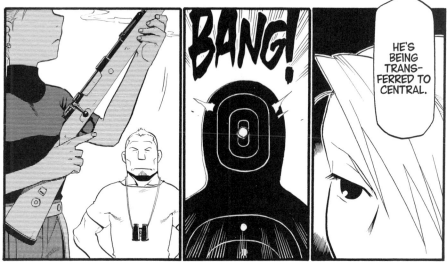

YES, SIR.

MASTER SERGEANT KAIN FUERY.

Yes, sir.

WARRANT OFFICER VATO FALMAN.

Sir.

SECOND LIEU-TENANT HEYMANS BREDA.

Yo.

WELL, THEN!

FIRST LIEU-TENANT RIZA HAWKEYE.

Here.

SECOND LIEU-TENANT JEAN HAVOC.

...ARE BEING TRANSFERRED TO CENTRAL.

THE FIVE OF YOU...

SAL UTE

Yes sir

I WON'T HEAR ANY OBJEC-TIONS.

YOU'RE COMING WITH ME.

WHAT?

ALMOST FORGOT! THERE'S JUST ONE PROBLEM, SIR!

OH.

YOU CAN FIND A NEW GIRL IN CENTRAL.

GLARE

DUMP HER.

So that's that.

Y'SEE, I JUST GOT A NEW GIRLFRIEND!

PAT

PAT

Ha ha ha!

CONSIDER YOURSELF LUCKY THAT YOU GOT OFF EASY!

IF YOU JUST STARTED GOING OUT, THEN YOUR RELATION-SHIP ISN'T TOO SERIOUS YET.

MAN, I DIDN'T KNOW IT WAS SO LATE.

SORRY, I DON'T HAVE ANY MONEY.

HEY! WHAT ABOUT YOU, SIR? IN THE ARMOR?

PAD PAD PAD

HOW CAN YOU BE SO COLD-HEARTED?!

PAD

D A S H

SHUT UP! GO GET A JOB!

How rude!

NONE OF THE ALCHE-MISTS I KNOW HAVE ANY MONEY.

TMP TMP TMP TMP TMP TMP TMP

PAD PAD PAD

PAD

OH, COME ON! AS A STATE ALCHEMIST, YOU MUST BE ROLLING IN DOUGH, RIGHT?

YOU'RE FAMOUS, AREN'T YOU, SIR? YOU'RE THE ALCHEMIST...

PAD

PAD PAD

NO NEED TO PLAY DUMB.

STOP

...WHO TRANSMUTED HIS BROTHER'S SOUL.

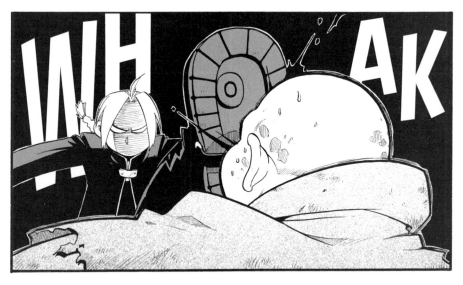

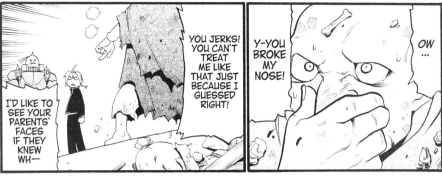

GRAB

SHF

PAT

WHY ARE YOU STILL TALKING, YOU—

LOOM

MISTER.

Eep!

GIVE IT A REST, OKAY?

FWIP

S... SORRY ABOUT THAT.

THAT WAS CHILD- ISH OF ME.

WEH HEH HEH.

YOU'RE THE ONES WHO TRANS- MUTED A SOUL!

YAH HAAH!! THERE'S NO MISTAK- ING IT NOW!

WEH HEH HEH.

GOOD JOB, BIDO!

YOU'RE REALLY SOMETHING ELSE!

THEY SAVED US THE TROUBLE OF LOOKING FOR THEM.

I DIDN'T THINK THEY'D COME ALL THE WAY OUT HERE TO DUBLITH.

GET THEM OVER HERE. TELL THEM IT'S AN EMERGENCY.

WHAT DO YOU WANT US TO DO, BOSS?

HERE'S YOUR USUAL PRESCRIPTION.

THANK YOU VERY MUCH.

IT'S NOT MY AREA OF EXPERTISE. WHY DO YOU ASK?

AMNESIA?

DOCTOR, DO YOU KNOW MUCH ABOUT **AMNESIA?**

THE MOST WELL-KNOWN METHOD IS TO USE HYPNOSIS TO RETRACE A PERSON'S MEMORIES BACK TO THE SUBCONSCIOUS.

A FRIEND OF MINE LOST A SMALL PORTION OF HIS MEMORY. I WAS HOPING THERE WAS SOME WAY I COULD HELP HIM.

A STRONG SHOCK, HUH?

I'VE ALSO HEARD THAT A STRONG SHOCK CAN MAKE OLD MEMORIES RESURFACE.

WHAT'S THE MATTER, BIG BROTHER?

Throw out your back?

OH NO!!

I TOTALLY FORGOT ABOUT THIS YEAR'S ASSESSMENT.

THIS ISN'T GOOD. NOT GOOD AT ALL...

I'VE BEEN SO BUSY LATELY I FORGOT ALL ABOUT IT!

EVERY YEAR WE HAVE TO PASS AN ASSESSMENT OR THEY'LL TAKE AWAY OUR LICENSE.

THE ANNUAL ASSESS-MENT FOR STATE ALCHE-MISTS!

THIS YEAR'S WHAT?

SURE HAVE!

I'VE BEEN MEANING TO GO TO HEAD-QUARTERS ANYWAY.

Feh!

Hello ?!

STOP !!

I'LL GO AHEAD AND LET MILITARY HQ KNOW YOU WON'T BE SHOWING UP.

GREAT! YOU CAN USE THIS OPPORTUNITY TO QUIT BEING A DOG OF THE MILITARY.

FWUMP

WAIT, BIG BROTHER! SOUTH HQ IS MUCH CLOSER THAN CENTRAL.

IT'S ONLY TWO STATIONS AWAY BY TRAIN.

GOT IT. THANKS, AL.

RUSTLE FWAP

YOU BE CAREFUL OUT THERE.

I WILL.

I'LL ONLY BE GONE TWO OR THREE DAYS.

RUSTLE FUMP

I'LL JUST WHIP SOME-THING UP ON THE TRAIN.

WHAT ABOUT YOUR REPORT?

TM TM TM TM

TM TM TM TM TM TM

HWAAAAAA

I'M OFF!

OKAY.

YOU SHOULDN'T BE PUSHING YOURSELF SO HARD WHEN YOUR WOUNDS HAVEN'T EVEN HEALED YET!

JUST WASH YOUR FACE!

AN ISHVALAN WARRIOR MUST TRAIN CONTINU- OUSLY—

SPLAT

YOU GOT A VISI- TOR.

MASTER !!

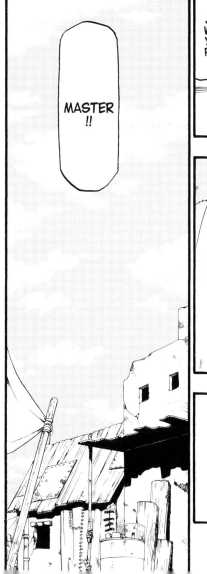

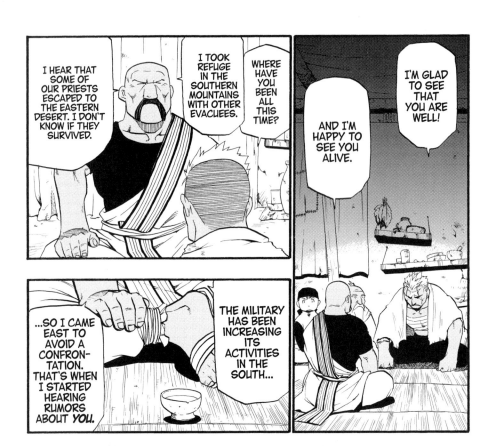

BUT WHAT YOU ARE DOING IS NOTHING BUT **SENSELESS REVENGE.**

I UNDER-STAND WHY YOU HATE THEM.

IT IS TRUE THAT STATE ALCHEMISTS ARE RESPONSIBLE FOR BURNING DOWN OUR VILLAGES.

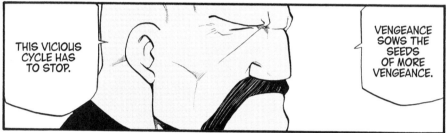

THIS VICIOUS CYCLE HAS TO STOP.

VENGEANCE SOWS THE SEEDS OF MORE VENGEANCE.

THIS IS A TIME OF TRIAL. WE MUST ENDURE.

DON'T MIND US.

HYUK HYUK HYUK

ONE OF YOU DESERT RATS WAS NICE ENOUGH TO TELL US THAT THERE'S AN INJURED MAN HERE WITH A BOUNTY ON HIS HEAD. HELL OF A BOUNTY TOO.

WE'RE GONNA BE RICH!

THAT'S OUR MAN, ALL RIGHT! THE ISHVALAN WITH THE X-SHAPED SCAR!

WHAT DID YOU SAY?!

EEP!

SO WHO...?

NO ONE HERE WOULD SELL OUT A FELLOW REFUGEE!

WE'LL SPLIT IT THREE WAYS, LIKE WE AGREED.

THANKS FOR THE TIP, YOKI.

WE TOOK YOU IN WHEN YOU DIDN'T HAVE ANY PLACE TO STAY!

WE TREATED YOU LIKE FAMILY!

YOKI, HOW COULD YOU?!!

EEHAA HA HA!!

I NEED THAT MONEY TO GET BACK ON MY FEET! I'LL USE IT TO RISE BACK TO THE TOP!

I'M NOT LIKE YOU AT ALL!

SH-SHUT UP! YOU PEOPLE LOST THE WAR! IT'S OVER!

EEK!

GLARE

TMP
TMP

TMP

STAY AWAY!

YOU GOTTA BELIEVE ME!

I DIDN'T MEAN NOTHIN', MAN!

STOP ...

TMP

TMP

N-NO!

WAIT!

WHAT ?!

THAT GUY WITH THE MUSTACHE— IT WAS ALL HIS IDEA!

AIEEEEE!!!

GLARE!

YOU'RE LEAVING?

CHAK

HW

YOUR OLDER BROTHER WILL BE SAD.

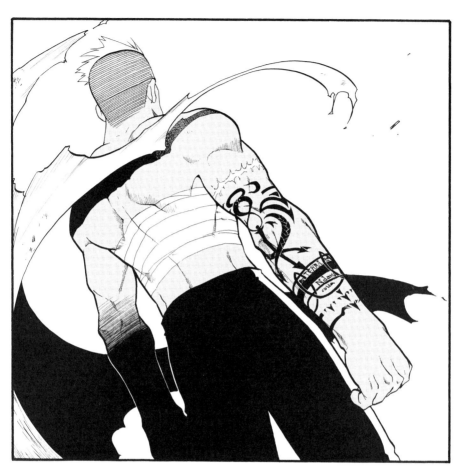

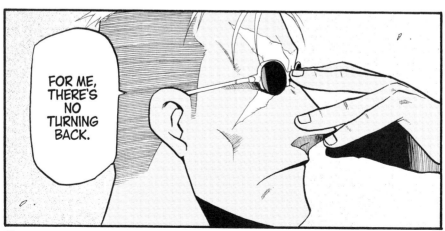

FOR ME, THERE'S NO TURNING BACK.

POFF

TUP TUP

MEAT

BEEF ...
PORK ...
CHICKEN ...
MAMMOTH ...

SWIF
SWIF

?

ALL RIGHT, WHO'S THE LITTER-BUG?

TBK, TBK

CRINK

68

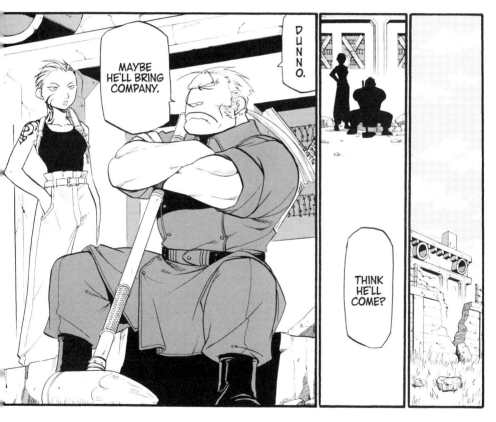

MAYBE HE'LL BRING COMPANY.

DUNNO.

THINK HE'LL COME?

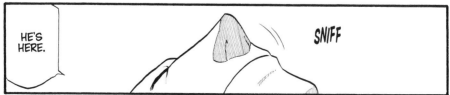

HE'S HERE.

SNIFF

IS HE ALONE?

HE'S PRETTY BRAVE. OR STUPID.

HE'S ALONE.

...AND YOU MIGHT FIND OUT ABOUT WHAT YOU WANT TO KNOW.

COME WITH US...

THEN LET'S GET TO THE POINT.

FOUR-TEEN.

HOW OLD ARE YOU?

BUT MY TEACHER SAID I'M NOT SUPPOSED TO GO WITH STRANGERS.

• • •

FOURTEEN-YEAR-OLDS SHOULD BE ABLE TO THINK AND ACT FOR THEMSELVES, RIGHT?

Uh-huh.

LISTEN, IF YOU'RE A *MAN*, THEN YOU SHOULD MAKE YOUR OWN DECISIONS!

NOW YOU'RE GETTIN' IT! SO JUST COME WITH US!

'Kay?

NO MORE OF THAT "TEACHER SAYS" CRAP! TELL US WHAT *YOU* WANT!

YOU'RE RIGHT! I *SHOULD* MAKE MY OWN DECISION!

72

AFTER THINKING FOR MYSELF...

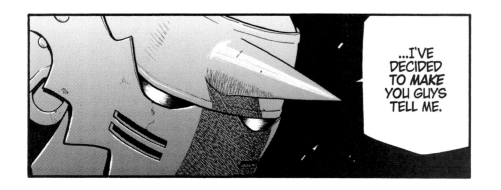

BRACE
FOR IT.

THEN WE NAB HIM. PIECE OF CAKE.

THERE'S NO WAY SOMEONE WHO'S NEVER BEEN HERE BEFORE COULD FIND HIS WAY THROUGH THIS PLACE.

EVENTUALLY HE'LL RUN INTO A DEAD END.

...

PIECE OF CAKE...

HMM...

I THOUGHT WE HAD THE HOME-COURT ADVANTAGE?!

WHAT THE HELL?!

BIG BROTHER AND I PLAYED A LOT OF HIDE-AND-SEEK HERE BACK WHEN WE WERE TRAINING.

THIS SURE BRINGS BACK MEMORIES.

TRA LA LA

HE DOESN'T HAVE TO WORRY ABOUT GETTING TIRED.

I SEE. I GUESS NOT HAVING A BODY HAS ITS ADVANTAGES.

WHAT?

THAT DAMN SUIT OF ARMOR JUST KEEPS RUNNING AND RUNNING. WILL HE EVER STOP AND FIGHT?!

HE'S PLANNING ON RUNNING US IN CIRCLES UNTIL WE'RE WORN OUT, THEN STOPPING TO FINISH US OFF.

!

TMPTMPTMPTMP

DOL- CETTO!

K TING

TNG

TNG

TNG

TNG

THAT LITTLE BRAT!

ZSHHH

Whoa!

ZSSSSH

USING THE BACK OF THE BLADE TO TRY TO STUN HIM DIDN'T WORK!

SINCE HE'S FIGHTING HAND TO HAND, AS LONG AS I KEEP MY DISTANCE, I SHOULD BE OKAY.

SWF

HE'S A TOUGH OPPONENT, ALL RIGHT.

SWF

I'D LOVE TO JUST CHOP THIS GUY IN HALF, BUT I HAVE MY ORDERS.

Grr!

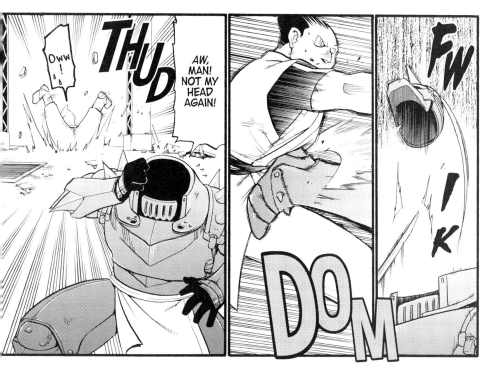

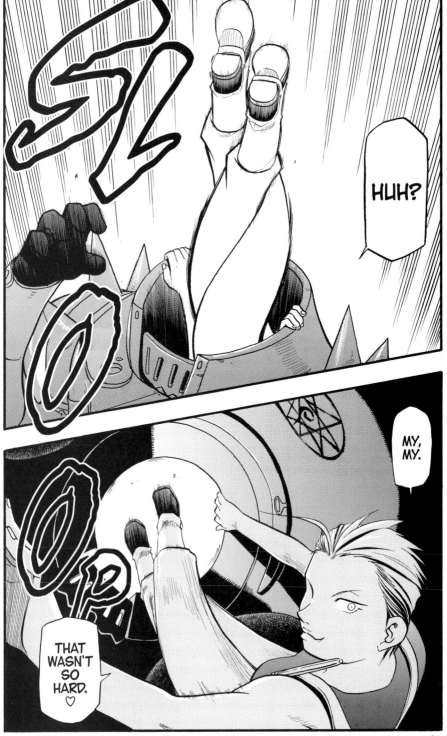

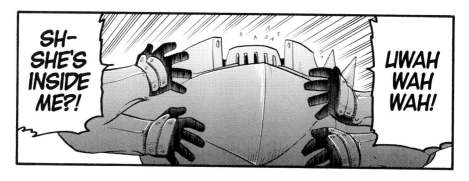

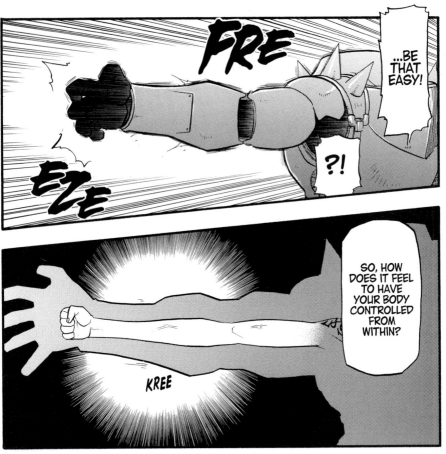

...BE THAT EASY!

FRE

EZE

?!

SO, HOW DOES IT FEEL TO HAVE YOUR BODY CONTROLLED FROM WITHIN?

KREE

HEH HEH. THIS ISN'T A CONTEST OF STRENGTH.

KRK

KRK

KRK

TRY ALL YOU WANT, YOU CAN'T CONTROL ME COMPLETELY. I'M STILL STRONGER THAN YOU.

KREEE

KRIK!

87

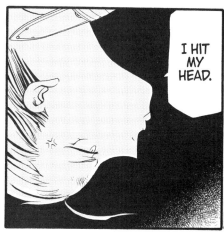

YOU KNOW, BOSS, I'M A LITTLE WORRIED...

WHAT COULD HE BE UP TO?!

HUH?

ALPHONSE ISN'T BACK YET?

MAYBE HE WAS KIDNAPPED.

LIKE THAT COULD EVER HAPPEN!

AHA HA HA HA HA HA HA HA

YEAH, RIGHT!

CHAPTER 27 **THE BEASTS OF DUBLITH**

SORRY ABOUT THIS.

I KNOW IT FEELS WEIRD WITH ME INSIDE, BUT YOU'VE JUST GOT TO DEAL WITH IT, OKAY?

I GOT GUARD DUTY.

THAT'S ALL RIGHT. I'M ALREADY USED TO IT.

YOU KNOW...

...YOUR BODY'S PRETTY NEAT.

IT'S THE ONLY THING THAT'S KEEPING ME IN THIS WORLD.

JUST DON'T TOUCH THE BLOOD RUNE IN THERE.

YOU'RE PRETTY UNUSUAL YOURSELF, AREN'T YOU, MISS?

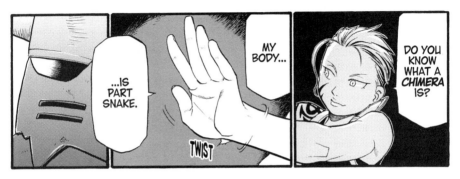

...IS PART SNAKE.

MY BODY...

TWIST

DO YOU KNOW WHAT A CHIMERA IS?

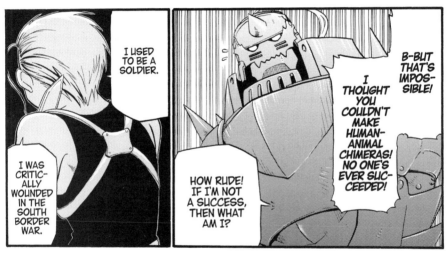

I USED TO BE A SOLDIER.

I WAS CRITIC-ALLY WOUNDED IN THE SOUTH BORDER WAR.

I THOUGHT YOU COULDN'T MAKE HUMAN-ANIMAL CHIMERAS! NO ONE'S EVER SUC-CEEDED!

B-BUT THAT'S IMPOS-SIBLE!

HOW RUDE! IF I'M NOT A SUCCESS, THEN WHAT AM I?

THAT'S...

...HOW I GOT LIKE THIS.

THE MILITARY DRAGGED MY HALF-DEAD BODY TO THEIR LABORATORIES AND USED ME IN THEIR EXPERIMENTS.

HEH HEH.

I CAN'T BELIEVE THE MILITARY WOULD DO THAT.

EXPERIMENTING ON PEOPLE, CHANGING YOUR BODY... IT'S TOO HORRIBLE FOR WORDS!

BUT THAT'S *AWFUL!*

"AWFUL"?

YEAH. THEY DIDN'T GIVE A DAMN WHAT WE WANTED.

TO THOSE SCIENTISTS, WE WERE JUST LAB RATS.

I GUESS IT *WAS* PRETTY CALLOUS.

THE LAST THING I REMEMBERED WAS HAVING HALF MY BODY BLOWN OFF BY A MINE, AND WHEN I WOKE UP I HAD THE BODY OF A SNAKE.

AND...

...YOU DON'T EVEN WANT TO KNOW WHAT THE FAILURES LOOKED LIKE.

...BECAUSE WE WERE SUR- VIVORS.

WE WERE THE SUCCESS STORIES. WE GOT A SECOND CHANCE AT LIFE...

AT LEAST I'M ALIVE.

IF THEY HADN'T PICKED ME, I WOULD'VE DIED ANYWAY.

HUMAN OR CHIMERA, IT DOESN'T MATTER IN THE END.

I DO NOT!!

JUST WATCH. HE RAISES ONE LEG WHEN HE PEES.

GUESS.

WHAT ANIMAL DID THEY COMBINE YOU WITH?

YEAH.

THAT HIM?

KTANG

NICE TO MEET YOU, KID.

Grr!

WHOA! COOL! HE REALLY IS EMPTY.

Hey!

POP

LET'S BE FRIENDS.

THE NAME'S GREED.

AN...

...OURO-BOROS TATTOO!

HUH? YOU KNOW ABOUT THESE?

AWW, DOESN'T MATTER.

WHICH ONE? WAS IT THAT HAG LUST? OR THAT LAZY-ASS SLOTH?

HUH! SO YOU MET ONE OF THE OTHERS?

I MET SOMEONE WEIRD IN CENTRAL WHO HAD THAT MARK.

BUT WE'RE NOT EXACTLY *GOOD* EITHER.

I WOULDN'T SAY THAT WE'RE *BAD*.

WHAT, ARE YOU SOME KIND OF "BAD GUYS"?

SO.

AL, ISN'T IT?

WHAT DOES IT FEEL LIKE TO BE NOTHING BUT A SOUL WITH A BODY THAT CAN NEVER DIE?

REMEMBER WHEN YOU FOUGHT A SERIAL KILLER BACK IN EAST CITY?

GA HA HA!! HOW DO I KNOW?!

HOW DO YOU KNOW THAT ABOUT ME?

THE COMMANDER IN CHARGE OF THE OPERATION PLACED A GAG ORDER ON THE INCIDENT. BUT...

PLENTY OF CIVILIANS AND SOLDIERS WERE ON THE SCENE, AND THEY SAW YOU.

...SECRETS HAVE A WAY OF GETTING OUT.

ANYWAY, I'VE GOT MY SOURCES.

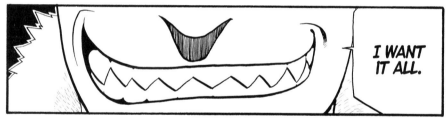

THE SECRET LIES INSIDE OF YOU.

AND MOST OF ALL... *ETERNAL LIFE!*

...TO FIND OUT THE SECRETS OF YOUR SOUL.

TRY TO REFUSE AND I'LL CUT YOU APART...

AND NOW YOU'RE GONNA HELP ME GET IT.

HUH?

YOU *ARE* A BAD GUY.

THAT'S TOO BAD.

SKRCH

YOU WERE SAYING?

YOU LET YOUR GUARD DOWN!

SKTCH

SKTCH

I CAN EASILY BREAK THESE CHAINS WITH ALCHEMY...

KRMBL

BANG

GRAB

?!

GRIND GRIND   GRIND

JUST CHILL.

OKAY?

SPIN   SPIN

FORGOT YOU WERE IN THERE.

OOPS! SORRY ABOUT THAT, MARTEL.

IF YOU REALLY WANNA KILL ME, THEN YOU GOTTA TRY HARDER— LIKE THIS.

BUT PARLOR TRICKS LIKE THESE AIN'T GONNA CUT IT.

I'LL GIVE YOU THAT.

HA HA HA! YOU GOT SPUNK, KID.

WHY DID YOU DO THAT?!

HE WAS YOUR...

W...

HUH?

FLINCH

...
FRIEND
?

SNAP

THAT'S HOW YOU KILL A GUY!

AH...

CRIK CRIK

UR...

OOH...

OH.

SORRY, BOSS.

HEY, ROA. COULDN'T YOU HAVE MADE IT A LITTLE BIT CLEANER?

CRIK CRAK

YOU CAN'T BE IMMOR-TAL?!

NO! YOU CAN'T BE...

...YOU CAN'T COME AT ME HALF-ASSED.

SNORT

SO, AS YOU CAN SEE...

EVEN WITH A BODY LIKE THIS, I'M NOT IMMORTAL.

YOU'RE RIGHT.

YOU'VE HEARD OF A HOMUNCULUS, RIGHT?

I WAS MADE TO LAST.

IT'S AN ARTIFICIAL HUMAN BEING.

I MIGHT LOOK YOUNG, BUT I'VE BEEN AROUND FOR CLOSE TO 200 YEARS.

THAT'S WHAT YOU'RE LOOKING AT RIGHT NOW.

A PERSON THAT'S NOT A PERSON.

HOW LITTLE YOU UNDERSTAND.

GA HA HA!!

THAT CAN'T BE! NO ONE'S **EVER** MADE A HOMUNCULUS! IT'S **IMPOSSIBLE!**

THERE'S ANOTHER WORLD OUTSIDE OF THE ONE YOU LIVE IN—A **SHADOW WORLD.** THINGS GO ON DOWN HERE THAT YOU PEOPLE IN THE LIGHT WOULD NEVER BELIEVE.

NOTHING IS IMPOSSIBLE.

YOU WERE TOLD THAT SUCCESSFUL CHIMERA DIDN'T EXIST, AND YET HERE THEY ARE.

YOU, WHO ONLY HAVE A SOUL.

THE FACT THAT **YOU** EXIST PROVES THAT, DOESN'T IT?

NOW TELL ME YOURS.

TELL ME WHAT THEY DID WITH YOUR SOUL.

I'VE TOLD YOU *MY* SECRET.

I DON'T REMEMBER HOW I GOT THIS BODY.

I CAN'T.

I'D TELL HIM IF I WERE YOU.

YOU DON'T WANT TO BE TAKEN APART AND TREATED LIKE A LAB ANIMAL, DO YOU?

...WHO PERFORMED THE TRANSMUTATION.

THEN ALL WE HAVE TO DO IS ASK THE PERSON...

SOMEONE ELSE PERFORMED THE ALCHEMY. I DON'T KNOW ANYTHING, HONEST.

114

GYAAA AAAAH!

HUG KRAK SNAP

117

HA HA HA HA!!

WA HA HA HA!!

Ahem.

What crummy timing...

I AM *HONORED* TO HAVE BEEN CHOSEN TO ESCORT THE FÜHRER-PRESIDENT ON HIS INSPECTION OF THE SOUTHERN HEADQUARTERS.

UH-HUH.

I'M SO GLAD TO SEE YOU'RE WELL!

OH, *THAT'S* ALL?

HERE, LET ME SEE THE FORM.

YEAH, BUT...

...I MISSED THE DEADLINE, SO IT'S GONNA TAKE THEM A WHILE TO PROCESS THE DOCU-MENTS.

YOU'RE HERE FOR YOUR ASSESS-MENT, ARE YOU?

YES, SIR.

MY SEAL, PLEASE.

Th...that can't be okay...

EDWARD ELRIC! HOW FORTUNATE YOU ARE!

ASSESS-MENT COM-PLETE!

Here.

YOU PASS!

ST AMP

NOT AT ALL! I'M JUST VISITING MY FORMER ALCHEMY TEACHER IN DUBLITH.

SO, DID YOU COME TO THE SOUTH AREA TO STIR UP TROUBLE?

HA HA HA

I'M LOOKING FORWARD TO SEEING YOU IN ACTION AGAIN, MY DEAR FULLMETAL ALCHEMIST!

RELAX! BASED ON WHAT I'VE SEEN OF YOUR PER-FORMANCE OVER THE YEARS, YOU WOULD HAVE PASSED WITH FLYING COLORS.

SKILLED, YES. (AND SCARY!)

HMM.

IF THIS PERSON TAUGHT *YOU*, THEN THEY MUST BE *VERY* SKILLED INDEED.

SWIP

DEVIL'S NEST, HUH?

SOME GUYS WHO HANG OUT AT A BAR CALLED THE *DEVIL'S NEST* WERE CARRYING "A BIG SUIT OF ARMOR" DOWNSTAIRS.

LET'S GO PAY THEM A VISIT.

YOU GUYS ARE CLASSIC.

OKAY, I HEAR YOU.

IF YOU STICK YOUR PRETTY NECK INTO PLACES IT DON'T BELONG, IT'S GONNA GET CUT.

YOU THE BROAD WHO'S BEEN ASKING TOO MANY QUESTIONS?

SO WHERE'S THE PERSON IN CHARGE?

STRIDE

YOU'D BETTER TURN AROUND BEFORE WE—

SH A

BAM

BAM!

NOW HOLD ON!!

DON'T TURN YOUR BACK ON US, YOU—

124

HE'S A BEAST! A REAL MONSTER!

SNAP

SNAP

SNAP

HE'S GOT *CROCODILE BLOOD* RUNNIN' THROUGH HIS VEINS!

...YOU WALKED INTO A *BAD* PART OF TOWN...

OGLE ♡

SEXY LADY...

...SO DON'T BLAME ME IF YOU GET HURT! ♡

OUCH!!

WHAMA

LUNGE

HE'S A MONSTER!!

AW, IT'S SWEET OF YOU TO CALL ME YOUR WOMAN, BUT YOU DON'T HAVE TO SAY IT SO LOUD. ♡

GET YOUR EYES OFF MY WOMAN, YOU CREEP!!

BIFF BAM BOOM WHACK

GRRRRR

OH, HONEY, YOU CAME?

DANGLE

WELL?

WHO'S GOING TO TELL US WHAT WE WANT TO KNOW?

MEOW

WE'LL NEVER RAT OUT OUR FRIENDS!

FACE OF DESPERATION

Mama!

GET 'EM!

CORNERED RAT

Y-YOU WISH!

IF YOU DON'T TELL ME, I'LL—

WHAT DID YOU DO WITH THE ARMOR BOY?!

SO THEN...

MEOW

DRIP

HEH! YOU'LL WHAT?

HUH?

GYAAAAH!!! GROSS!! EWW!!

BLEGH

I'LL VOMIT BLOOD ALL OVER YOU.

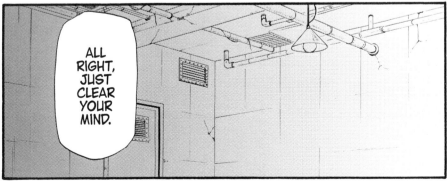

ALL RIGHT, JUST CLEAR YOUR MIND.

GO BACK... BACK TO THAT DAY WHEN YOUR SOUL WAS TRANSMUTED.

FLICKER

THINK BACK TO WHEN YOU WERE TEN.

JUST LIKE THAT.

THAT'S RIGHT.

LOOK INTO THE FLAME.

SIGH

NOPE! NOT WORKING.

I CAN DO A LITTLE ALCHEMY MYSELF.

JUST TAKE HIM APART AND LET ME ANALYZE HIM.

WHAT A WASTE OF TIME.

I DON'T KNOW, BOSS. THIS IS MY FIRST TIME TRYING IT ON A GUY LIKE HIM.

YOU SURE YOU'RE DOING IT RIGHT? I WAS CERTAIN HYPNOSIS WOULD DO THE TRICK.

128

I DON'T WANT TO BE DISSECTED BY *AMATEURS.*

IF YOU'RE GOING TO DO THAT, YOU SHOULD AT LEAST BRING IN SOMEONE WITH THE SKILLS OF A STATE ALCHEMIST.

Hmph...

WHOA! KID'S GOT A POINT.

BUT —!!

GRAB

HE'S GOT NERVES OF STEEL.

HMPH!

I *LIKE* GUYS LIKE YOU.

...IS YOU ACTING LIKE YOU'RE NOT AFRAID!

WHAT I **DON'T** LIKE...

CALM DOWN.

YOU WANT THAT?

HE'S OUR ONLY LEAD.

I CAN *RIP YOU APART* WITH MY **BARE HANDS.**

SNIK

RMB

...

RUMBLE

WHAT'S THAT NOISE?

RRMMB

?

THERE'S ONLY **ONE THING** THAT I'M AFRAID OF.

RMBL

RMM

AND SPEAKING OF THAT THING...

...HERE IT COMES.

BAM

HUH?

EEE

KREE

132

YOU STUPID MORON!

HEY! WE'RE THE ONES ASKING QUESTIONS AROUND HERE!

WHO THE HELL ARE YOU?!

I...I... I'M... S... SORRY !!!

HOW THE HELL COULD YOU LET YOURSELF GET KIDNAPPED?!

CHAPTER 28 **A FOOL'S COURAGE**

YOU SURE LIKE SURPRISES, DON'T YOU, LADY?

...

YOUR FINGERS... ARE THEY BROKEN?

KRIK KRIK

SO DO I.

KRIK

...!!

I DON'T LIKE FIGHTING WOMEN.

GIVE IT A REST, WILL YOU?

KRIK

TEACHER!!

IT TAKES MORE THAN YOU CAN DEAL OUT TO SCRATCH THIS HIDE.

SHRIK

AIN'T THAT THE TRUTH.

YOU'VE GOT A RATHER UNIQUE BODY.

?

NO. HE HASN'T COME BACK YET.

WHERE'S ED?

DID MY BROTHER COME WITH YOU?!

AH!

142

DOL-CETTO!!

SLAM GUFF

WHY DON'T I JUST SLICE THIS BROAD UP—

OH, TO HELL WITH THIS, GREED!

WHY DO YOU NEED TO KNOW ABOUT THAT?

I JUST WANNA KNOW HOW HIS SOUL WAS TRANSMUTED.

HOW ABOUT *THIS*?

GRAB

C'MON! IT AIN'T THAT HARD!

Meanwhile, Sig...

We'll show you a good time!

I got caught...

Let's have a drink!

I love big, strong men!

SO YOU WANNA MAKE A *DEAL*, HUH?

I'LL SHOW *HIM* HOW TO CREATE A HOMUNCULUS...

...AND HIS BROTHER WILL TEACH *ME* HOW TO TRANSMUTE A SOUL.

GOT IT?

I'D LIKE TO KEEP THINGS CIVIL.

LET'S CALL IT AN *EQUIVALENT EXCHANGE.*

PLEASE! BRING ED HERE!

TEACH-ER!!

DON'T MAKE ME—

YOU THINK I'M GONNA MAKE DEALS WITH A *KID-NAPPER?*

YOUR NAME'S *GREED,* RIGHT?

THIS IS THE CHANCE WE'VE BEEN WAITING FOR.

PLEASE JUST GET HIM.

I DON'T LIKE SAYING THINGS LIKE THIS.

AS AN ALCHEMIST, I PREFER TO CREATE THINGS.

...I WON'T HESITATE TO DESTROY YOU.

IF ANYTHING HAPPENS TO THAT BOY...

I'M GOING.

UH, THANKS.

WOW. YOUR TEACHER'S REALLY SOMETHIN' ELSE.

...

LET ME EX-PLAIN!

IT'S NOT WHAT IT LOOKS LIKE!

HEY!

WHAT THE HELL ARE YOU DOING WITH THESE WOMEN?!

EEEK! WAAAH!

NOW ARRIVING IN DUBLITH.

DUBLITH STATION.

PHEW. IT SURE IS HOT OUT HERE.

BUT AT LEAST THE ASSESSMENT DIDN'T TAKE AS LONG AS I EXPECTED.

HELL OF A TOWN, THIS DUBLITH. *HELL* OF A TOWN!

RUMMAGE

I HOPE THIS YEAR WE CAN FINALLY GET OUR BODIES BACK.

I can't take it anymore...

GLEAM

I MERELY USED THE SECRET TRACKING SKILLS THAT HAVE BEEN PASSED DOWN IN THE ARMSTRONG FAMILY FOR GENERATIONS!

I'M HERE TO SEE IZUMI. FETCH HER FOR ME, WOULD YOU, MY GOOD MAN?

PORK TENDERLOIN, 128 CENZ FOR 100 GRAMS!

CHICKEN BREAST, 160 CENZ!

BEEF SHOULDER, 200 CENZ!

I'VE HEARD THAT SHE'S QUITE SKILLED IN THE ART OF ALCHEMY.

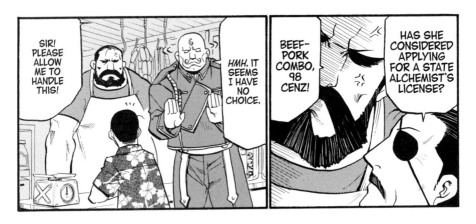

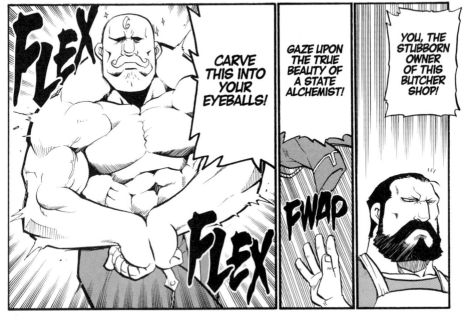

INHALE

RMM
RMM
RMM
RMM
RMM

RMM

RMM

HRM
?!

CLASP

HUH?! AL WAS WHAT?!

WHOA! IT'S A FRIEND-SHIP FORGED FROM MUSCLE!

HA HA HA HA HA

BUT WHY?! DO THEY WANT A *RANSOM*?!

THINGS GOT A LITTLE COMPLI-CATED.

WHAT DO YOU MEAN, "KIDNAPPED"? WHAT HAPPENED?!

WHO IN THE WORLD WOULD WANT TO KNOW ABOUT SOMETHING LIKE THAT?

IN OTHER WORDS, THEY WANT ME TO BRING YOU TO THEM.

THEY WANT INFORMATION ABOUT AL'S SOUL.

A MAN WITH AN OUROBOROS TATTOO ON HIS HAND NAMED GREED.

REDEMPTOR ETMEDI ATOR

IT'S HARD TO BELIEVE, BUT APPARENTLY HE'S A REAL HOMUNCULUS.

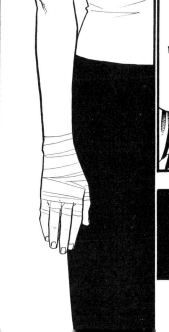

I WISH I WAS. THE GUY'S DEFINITELY NOT A NORMAL HUMAN BEING.

YOU'RE KIDDING, RIGHT?

HE CAUGHT ME OFF GUARD, THAT'S ALL.

IT'S NOTHING.

OH, THIS?

TEACHER, DID HE DO THAT TO YOUR HAND?

TEACH-ER. I'M GONNA GO MEET THIS GUY.

BY YOUR-SELF?!

I'LL BE FINE! I MEAN, ALL THEY WANT IS INFORMATION!

YOU IDIOT! I'M NOT LETTING YOU GO INTO SUCH A DANGEROUS PLACE BY YOURSELF!

I'M GOING ALONE.

THIS PROBLEM IS AL'S AND MINE.

154

RIGHT?

IT'S NOT LIKE THEY'RE GONNA TRY TO **KILL** US OR ANYTHING!

WAVE

ALL RIGHT, ALL RIGHT! DO WHATEVER YOU WANT!

...

SO DON'T WORRY.

EVERYTHING WILL BE FINE!

JUST MAKE SURE YOU COME HOME IN TIME FOR DINNER.

...

YES, MA'AM!

Y...

KLAK

Phew!

I WONDER WHAT SHE'S MAKING FOR DINNER, ANYWAY?

DEVIL'S NEST...

CRUMPLE

AND YOU MUST BE EDWARD ELRIC, RIGHT?

ARE YOU GREED?

IT WOULD'VE BEEN A LOT EASIER IF WE ONLY NEEDED THIS KID IN THE ARMOR.

SORRY TO DRAG YOU DOWN HERE.

ARE YOU FOR REAL?

THAT'S A PRETTY BOLD CLAIM.

A HOMUN- CULUS, RIGHT?

BE CAREFUL, BIG BROTHER!

THIS GUY IS A—

IF YOU WANT, I'LL PROVE IT TO YOU...

...ON SECOND THOUGHT, I DON'T THINK SO.

It's too messy.

I MAKE IT A MATTER OF PRINCIPLE NEVER TO LIE.

...HE'LL TELL YOU HOW TO MAKE A HOMUNCULUS IF YOU TELL HIM HOW YOU TRANSMUTED MY SOUL.

HE SAYS...

YUP!

I HEAR YOU GUYS ARE INTERESTED IN CREATING BODIES.

IT'S A FAIR TRADE, RIGHT?

AN EQUIVA-LENT EXCHANGE?

UH... BIG BROTHER?

HOW DARE YOU, YOU CROOK?!

RRRING RRRING

I DON'T CARE WHAT YOU AND THE OTHER MEMBERS OF THE OUROBOROS ARE SCHEMING...

ARE YOU REALLY THAT STUPID?!

DON'T MAKE ME LAUGH!!!

AND NOW YOU WANT AN "EQUIVALENT EXCHANGE"?!

...BUT YOU KIDNAPPED MY BROTHER AND HURT MY TEACHER!

YOU WANNA KNOW ABOUT SOULS?! I'M NOT GONNA TELL YOU ANYTHING!

YOU ARE, WITHOUT A DOUBT, THE VILEST CREATURES ON THE FACE OF THE EARTH!

SHUDDER

SHUDDER SHUDDER

IN OTHER WORDS, I'M TAKING IT ALL AND GIVING YOU NOTHING!!!

I'LL CRUSH YOU CREEPS! I'LL SMASH YOU! IF I WANT YOUR SECRETS, I'LL FORCE YOU TO TELL ME!

NEXT!

BRATS WHO WON'T *LISTEN* NEED TO BE *TAUGHT.*

KLANG

TA

TMP!

GIVE UP, BOY. IT'S USELESS!

YOU CAN'T EVEN *SCRATCH* ME WITH THAT LETTER OPENER!!

THMM

THMM

YOU LEFT YOUR HEAD WIDE OPEN.

BLORSH

Whoa!!

VOOM

YOU CAN'T GET THROUGH MY SHIELD, AND EVEN IF YOU DO, IT WON'T MATTER.

DO YOU UNDERSTAND WHAT YOU'RE DEALING WITH NOW, KID?

DO THE EXCHANGE. THAT'S THE **SMART** THING TO DO.

LOOK. I KNOW YOUR TYPE.

...

...BUT TOTALLY LOSES HIS COOL WHEN HIS BROTHER OR SOMEONE GETS HURT. YOUR STEREOTYPICAL STOIC HERO.

YOU'RE THE KIND OF GUY WHO DOESN'T MIND GETTING THE CRAP BEAT OUT OF HIM...

YOU CAN'T KEEP REGEN-ERATING *FOREVER.*

I'LL JUST ATTACK YOU WHERE YOU DON'T HAVE ANY ARMOR, THAT'S ALL.

I'LL GET HIM BACK AFTER I BEAT YOU.

ARE YOU GOING TO LET YOUR *STUBBORNNESS* KEEP YOU FROM YOUR ONE SHOT AT THE INFO YOU NEED— AND GETTING YOUR BROTHER BACK?

YOU IDIOT.

SHM

SHM

SHM

SHM

SHM

SORRY... I WASN'T GIVING IT MY *ALL* UP TILL NOW.

GA HA HA HA !!

I DON'T LIKE TO SHOW PEOPLE THIS BECAUSE IT TAKES AWAY FROM MY SEXY GOOD LOOKS.

SHM

SHM

SHM

SHM

SHM

LIGH...

YOU OKAY, DOLCET-TO?

Put me down!!

RMMB

!

SNIFF

IT'S OKAY, LITTLE BUDDY.

I've been losing a lot lately.

PAT

LIGH... OW!

THAT LITTLE SNOT!

I DON'T LIKE THE SMELL OF THIS.

RRGH!!

?

WHAT IS IT?

SNIFF SNIFF

178

BLAM

BLAM BLAM

TROMP

TROMP

TROMP

TROMP

TR OMP

I'LL NEVER GO BACK TO THE LAB!

BANG BANG

YOU BAS-TARDS...

LEVEL TWO.

BL

AM

Glk !

BASEMENT LEVEL ONE SECURED.

THE REAR EXIT IS BLOCKED TOO.

TUG

THEY'VE COMPLETELY OVERRUN THE TOP FLOOR.

I'M SURE HE'LL BE FINE ON HIS OWN.

WHAT ABOUT GREED?

DON'T LET YOUR GUARD DOWN.

THANKS.

ARE YOU DEAD YET?

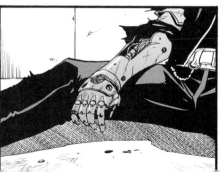

WE'VE GOT TO PROTECT THIS LEVEL WITH OUR LIVES UNTIL GREED GETS HERE.

Peh!

YEAH, YEAH...

I'LL BE SURE TO NOT DIE UNTIL THEN.

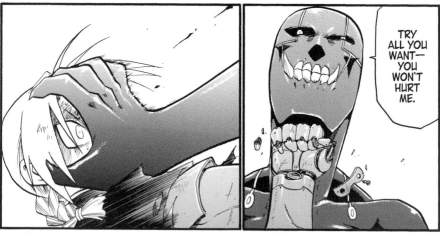

WELL, THEN.

READY TO TELL ME THE SECRETS OF SOUL TRANS- MUTA- TION?

HEFT

...!!

EH?

...

NOW I CAN THINK MORE CLEARLY.

I LOST SOME OF THE BLOOD THAT HAD RUSHED TO MY HEAD.

WHAT?

THANKS.

CAN YOU BELIEVE MY HAND STILL WORKS AFTER ALL THIS?

I HAVE THE WORLD'S GREATEST MECHANIC...

KRRRK

CL

GRRR

AP

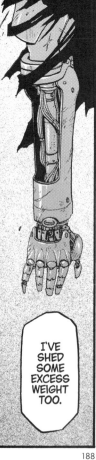

I'VE SHED SOME EXCESS WEIGHT TOO.

THAT WAS NONE OTHER THAN THE ULTIMATE BLOCKING TECHNIQUE THAT HAS BEEN PASSED DOWN IN THE ARMSTRONG FAMILY FOR GENERATIONS!!

TA DA A AA AAA

SHRK

TIME
TO GET
SERIOUS.

I SEE.

UH...

I GUESS *ORDINARY* METHODS WON'T WORK THIS TIME.

CLONK

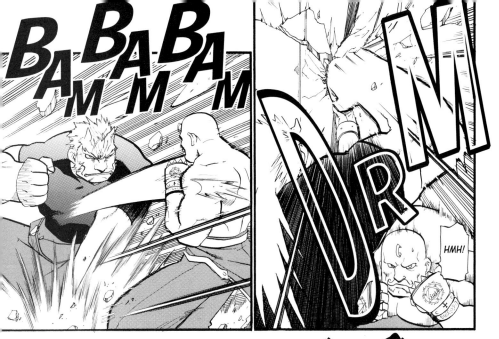

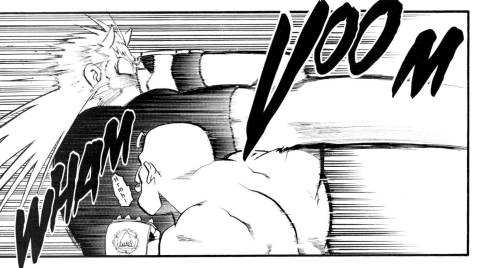

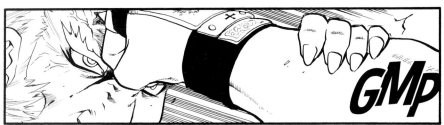

198

SL AM

MAJOR ARM-STRONG.

YOUR BLOWS ARE AS POWERFUL AS EVER.

FLICK

HEH HEH.

IT'S BEEN QUITE A WHILE SINCE I'VE BEEN IN SUCH A BLOOD-BOILING MELEE!

...A SOLDIER IN THE ISHVALAN EXTERMINA-TION CAMPAIGN.

I WAS ALSO...

SO WE WERE ONCE ALLIES.

HMH.

200

THEN, THE FOLKS AT THE BAR ARE ALREADY...

HE GAVE THE ORDER TO KILL THE ISHVALANS.

HE MUST BE PLANNING TO WIPE US ALL OUT.

YOU KNOW WHAT THAT MEANS, DON'T YOU?

SHNK

HRM.

ROA! WE'RE OUT-NUMBERED AND OUT-GUNNED!

O... OKAY...

TO THE EMERGENCY ESCAPE!

psst

LET'S GO.

WHAT'S GOING ON HERE, MAJOR ARMSTRONG?

DOLCETTO!!

MY ORDERS WERE TO KILL EVERYONE BUT THE TARGETS I SPECIFIED.

FWIP

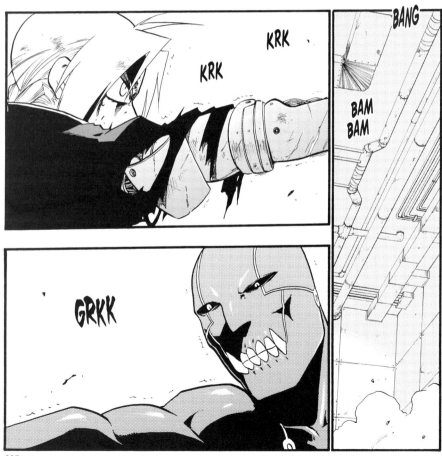

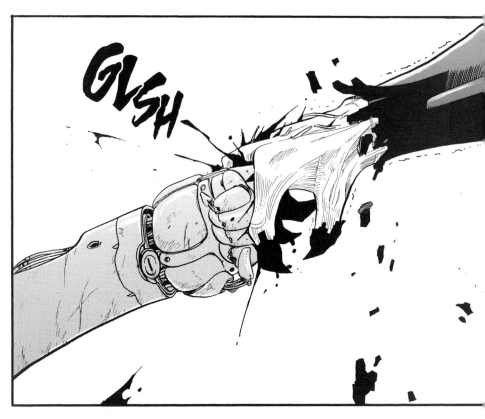

207

WHAT WAS THAT FOR?

I TOLD YOU, THAT WON'T—

THE SAME MOVE AGAIN?

WHAT?!

SHU

NK

FMP

GRAAHH!!!

WHAT DID YOU DO TO MY SHIELD?

NNGH...

AND I THOUGHT, "WHAT'S AN ELEMENT IN THE BODY THAT COULD BECOME A SHIELD THAT'S STRONGER THAN STEEL?"

IT WAS EASY ENOUGH ONCE I THOUGHT ABOUT IT. YOU CAN'T MAKE SOMETHING OUT OF NOTHING.

THEREFORE YOUR "SHIELD" IS BEING CREATED FROM SOMETHING.

YOU TOLD ME YOURSELF THAT YOU'RE CREATED FROM THE SAME BIOLOGICAL MATERIAL AS HUMANS.

CARBON!

THE SUBSTANCE THAT MAKES UP ONE-THIRD OF OUR BODIES...

FOR EXAMPLE, COMPARE THE LEAD FROM A PENCIL WITH A DIAMOND.

URGH...

THE HARDNESS OF CARBON VARIES DEPENDING ON HOW THE ATOMS ARE COMBINED.

SHM SHM

SHM SHM

SHM

ONCE I UNDERSTAND THE CHEMISTRY AT WORK, IT'S A SIMPLE MATTER OF ALCHEMY.

THWAK

K

K

YOU'RE GOOD! THIS IS MORE FUN THAN I THOUGHT!

HA HA !!

AND —!

SLAP

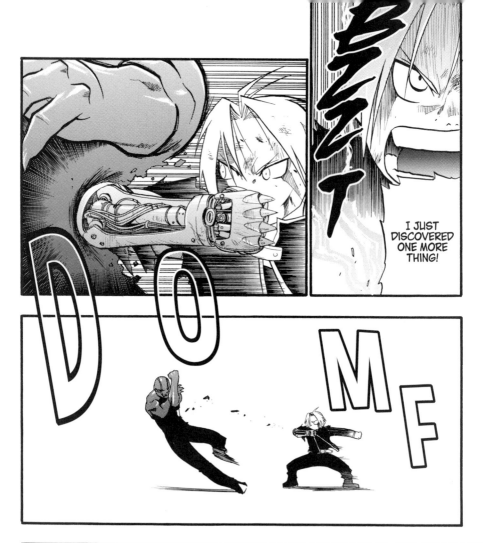

I JUST DISCOVERED ONE MORE THING!

YOU CAN'T HARDEN YOUR BODY AND REGENERATE AT THE SAME TIME!

GUGH

RRIP RRIP

I LIKE YOU, KID!

BUT I DON'T THINK I WANT TO FIGHT YOU ANYMORE.

HA HA HA!!

I THOUGHT YOU WERE JUST A HOTHEADED BRAT, BUT I GUESS I WAS WRONG.

GRIN

SORRY. GOTTA RUN!

HUH?

WE'VE FOUND THE BOY!!

SL AM

HEY!

HOW OLD ARE YOU?

I'LL BE 60 THIS YEAR.

HUH?

WHEN YOU GET OLD, YOUR BODY DOESN'T MOVE THE WAY YOU WANT IT TO.

SHRK

OLD MAN... YOU SHOULD RETIRE.

SO I JUST WANT TO GET THIS TIRESOME JOB DONE AND GO HOME.

TMP

217

219

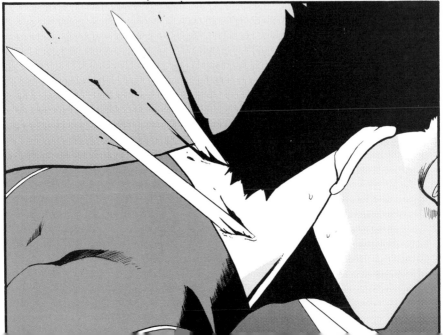

YOU KNOW...

...I DON'T HAVE YOUR ULTIMATE SHIELD...

...OR THE ULTIMATE SPEAR THAT CAN CUT THROUGH ANYTHING.

Why

you

CAN YOU GUESS?

SO YOU'RE PROBABLY WONDERING HOW I DISTINGUISHED MYSELF ON THE FIELD OF BATTLE WITH BULLETS WHIZZING ALL AROUND ME.

ZM

ZM

ZM

ZM

ZM

ZM

ZM

ZM

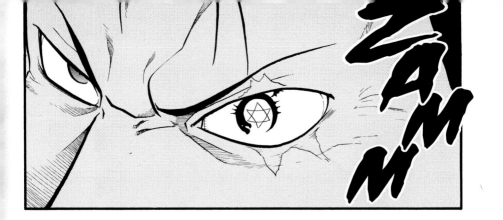

JUST AS YOU HAVE THE ULTIMATE SHIELD...

...I HAVE THE ULTIMATE EYE.

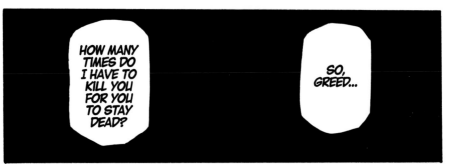

HOW MANY TIMES DO I HAVE TO KILL YOU FOR YOU TO STAY DEAD?

SO, GREED...

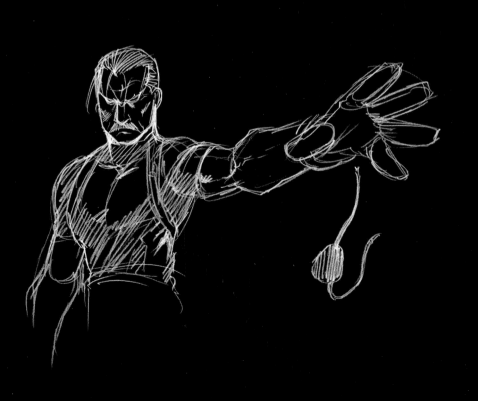

225

CHAPTER 30 THE TRUTH INSIDE THE ARMOR

LOOK AT ALL THIS MESS.

WHICH SIDE?

THEY'RE NOT HUMAN.

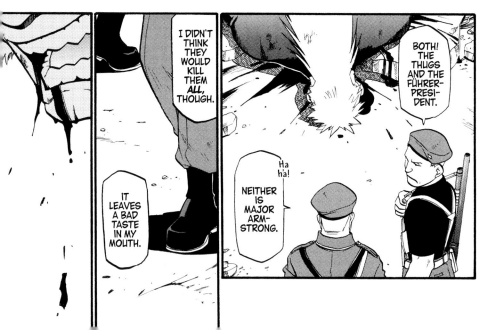

I DIDN'T THINK THEY WOULD KILL THEM *ALL*, THOUGH.

IT LEAVES A BAD TASTE IN MY MOUTH.

BOTH! THE THUGS AND THE FÜHRER-PRESIDENT.

Ha ha!

NEITHER IS MAJOR ARM-STRONG.

WHOA!

CHAK

CHAK

WHY, YOU —!

I THOUGHT YOU WERE DEA—

DOL-CETTO...

OW OW OW...

PTOO

LET'S
GO.

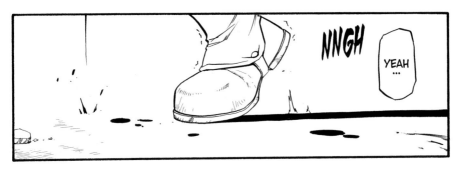

NNGH

YEAH
...

RM
RM
RM
RM
RM
RM
RM
RM

BAM
B-BAM
BAM
B-BAM

IT'S TOO DARK FOR ME TO SEE ANYTHING.

I DON'T KNOW.

CRASH
SLAM

SLAM!

WHAT'S GOING ON?! WHERE'S GREED?

SHH...H

SOUNDS LIKE THE FIGHTING HAS STOPPED.

TAK

!

I CAN'T LET YOU! YOU'LL BE KILLED!

C'MON, DAMMIT! OPEN UP!

NNGH?!

TH OK

NO! STAY DOWN!

SHING

LET ME OUT!

NO MEANS NO!

DAMN ... YOU ...

GLK

HM?

HOW MANY TIMES WILL IT TAKE FOR YOU TO STAY DEAD?

YOU'VE DIED FIFTEEN TIMES ALREADY.

STAGGER

SNAP

SHE'S STILL IN THERE, RIGHT?

SHUNK

WE'RE COUNTING ON YOU.

GET HER OUT OF HERE.

!

HEY...

BANG BANG

NO!! YOU CAN'T COME OUT RIGHT NOW!

SHUT UP!! YOU CAN'T KEEP ME HERE!

BANG

CLANG

CLANG

BANG

DO YOU EXPECT ME TO STAND BY AND LET MY FRIENDS DIE?!

I CAN'T LET YOU OUT!

I MADE A PROMISE!

OPEN, DAMN YOU!!

BANG

I CAN'T ...

...LET YOU OUT HERE!

HOW PATHET- IC.

FEELING PITY FOR YOUR PAWNS?

HOW COULD YOU DO THIS TO THEM? THEY WERE MY PEOPLE.

WHOA THERE, BRADLEY.

SPSH

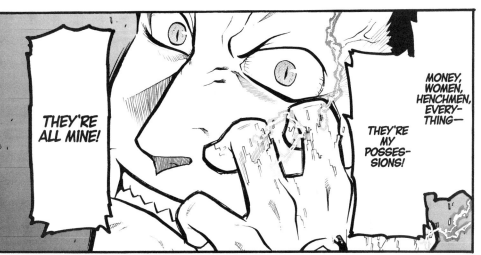

CLANK

I NEED TO ESCAPE ...

I...

ARE YOU HURT?

DO YOU NEED HELP?

YOU'RE EDWARD'S YOUNGER BROTHER, AREN'T YOU?

SLISH

HOLD IT.

I'M FINE.

N-NO, SIR!

HM?

RGH ...!

...SO IF YOU'LL EXCUSE ME...

I CAN FIND MY WAY OUT ON MY OWN...

N...

GRR
RR
RR

NO, MARTEL!

STOP
IT!

GRRK

!

GRAB

STOP—

DAMN YOU, BRAD-LEY!

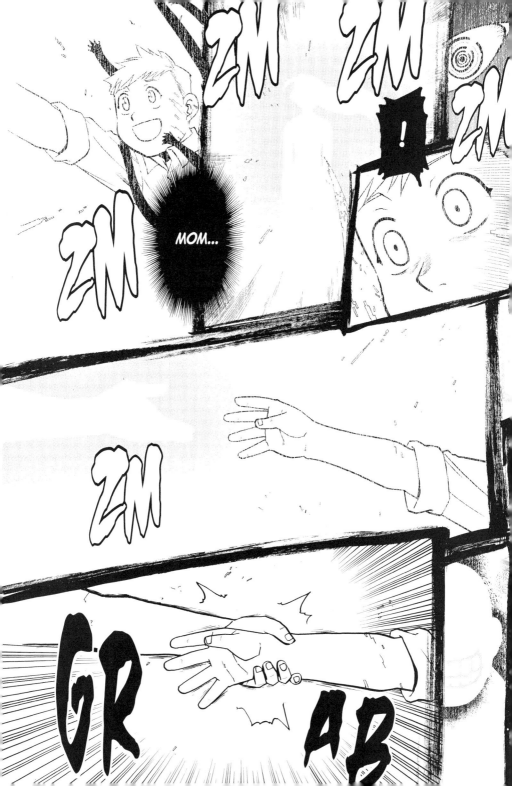

AL!!

E...
ED?

CLANG
CLANG CLANG

C'MON!
SAY
SOME-
THING!

OH...

WHY IS THERE BLOOD ON YOU?

ARE YOU OKAY?!

I COULDN'T HELP HER...

WE OPENED YOU UP AND PULLED HER OUT.

254

NO, WE DIDN'T.

DID YOU...

...MAKE ANY **DEALS** WITH THE MAN WITH THE OUROBOROS TATTOO?

NOTHING. HE DIDN'T ASK US ANYTHING ABOUT MILITARY AFFAIRS.

DID YOU SHARE ANY INFORMATION WITH HIM?

IF YOU MADE ANY **DEALS** WITH THEM OR SHARED ANY OF YOUR **EXPERTISE**, I'LL EXECUTE YOU BOTH RIGHT NOW.

IT'S NOT YOUR MILITARY KNOWLEDGE..

...I'M CONCERNED ABOUT.

!

CHAK

OF COURSE NOT.

ANY MORE QUESTIONS?

SO I ASK YOU AGAIN, DID YOU SAY **ANYTHING** TO THOSE PEOPLE THAT MIGHT CAUSE **PROBLEMS** FOR MY MILITARY?

IS THERE ANY CONNECTION BETWEEN THE TWO?

YOUR STEEL ARM AND YOUR BROTHER'S ARMOR BODY...

YOU'RE AN HONEST KID.

TAKE GOOD CARE OF YOUR BROTHER.

OH, AND ED...

ALL RIGHT, MEN. PULL OUT.

SCRUB

SCRUB

SCRUB

SCRUB
SCRUB

ALL DONE! GOOD AS NEW.

CLUNK

YOU OKAY, AL?

UH... UH-HUH.

I'M JUST IN A DAZE, THAT'S ALL.

NO!

IT'S NOT ABOUT THAT.

AL, IT'S NOT YOUR FAULT.

I GOT IT BACK. THE **MEMORY** OF WHEN MY BODY WAS TAKEN AWAY.

BUT I DIDN'T FIND OUT ANYTHING ABOUT TRANSMUTING HUMAN BODIES.

UH, IT WAS PRETTY WEIRD!

Kinda like this.

W-WHAT WAS IT LIKE?!

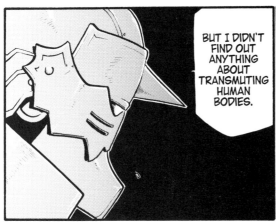

I SEE...

NO. THAT'S NOT TRUE.

I GUESS WE HAVEN'T MADE ANY PROGRESS, AFTER ALL.

THE PEOPLE WITH THE OUROBOROS TATTOOS WHO WERE MAKING PHILOSOPHER'S STONES...

DO YOU REMEMBER WHAT HAPPENED AT THE HOSPITAL IN CENTRAL?

SO WHY DID HE HAVE TO *KILL* THEM ALL?

...AND THAT HE WANTED TO GET TO THE BOTTOM OF IT.

THE FÜHRER-PRESIDENT SAID THAT THERE WAS SOME KIND OF CONSPIRACY GOING ON IN THE MILITARY...

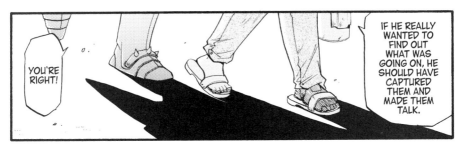

YOU'RE RIGHT!

IF HE REALLY WANTED TO FIND OUT WHAT WAS GOING ON, HE SHOULD HAVE CAPTURED THEM AND MADE THEM TALK.

WE SHOULD STAY CLOSER TO THE MILITARY FOR A WHILE.

IT SEEMS STRANGE THAT THE FÜHRER-PRESIDENT HIMSELF WOULD LEAD A MASSIVE OPERATION AGAINST SUCH A SMALL NUMBER OF PEOPLE.

THE PIECES JUST AREN'T ADDING UP.

SHUT UP! IF YOU WANT TO EAT, THEN ROLL UP YOUR SLEEVES AND GET TO WORK!

TEACHER, WE'RE HUNGRY!!

LET'S GO EAT!

ALL RIGHT, NOW THAT THAT'S SETTLED...

YEAH! WE MIGHT BE ABLE TO GET SOME INFORMATION ON THE PHILOSOPHER'S STONE!

CLONK

...AND ALL I DID WAS GO SHOPPING FOR THINGS THAT I'LL NEED AT HOME.

THIS IS MY FIRST DAY OFF SINCE I GOT TRANSFERRED TO CENTRAL...

GONG GONG

GONG

TAK TAK

TAK

TAK

KLAK

MISSING PERSON

TAK

KLAK

TAK

KLAK

HEY, LADY. IT'S **DANGEROUS** TO BE OUT ALONE THIS LATE AT NIGHT.

HOWS ABOUT I WALK YOU HOME?

THANKS FOR THE ADVICE.

BUT I'M FINE.

THERE'S ALL SORTS OF DANGEROUS CHARACTERS IN THESE PARTS...

NO NEED TO BE COY, LADY.

GEH HEH

LIKE BARRY THE CHOPPER!!!

HA HA HA HA!

FWP

Tch!

BLAM BLAM BLAM BLAM

WHAT THE -?!

AIEE!!

BA. NG

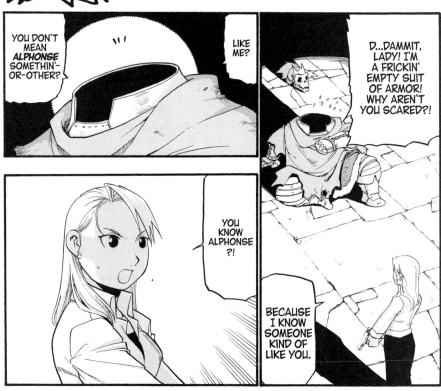

YOU DON'T MEAN *ALPHONSE* SOMETHIN'-OR-OTHER?

LIKE ME?

D...DAMMIT, LADY! I'M A FRICKIN' EMPTY SUIT OF ARMOR! WHY AREN'T YOU SCARED?!

YOU KNOW ALPHONSE?!

BECAUSE I KNOW SOMEONE KIND OF LIKE YOU.

WHO ARE YOU?! HOW DO YOU KNOW ALPHONSE?!

YOU GOT MOXIE, LADY. I LIKE THAT! ♡

CLONK

GEH HEH HEH HEH. YOU A FRIEND OF HIS?

VOLUME 5 / END

FULLMETAL EDITION

FULLMETAL ALCHEMIST

CONCEPT SKETCHES

05

エルリック兄弟の

師匠

これ！

ドレッド

連載開始頃、そのうち
こんなキャラ出ますよ〜と
担当さんにFAXしたやつ。

師匠は 外観 固まるの 早かったなぁ

From around when we began serialization of Fullmetal Alchemist in the manga magazine. I sent a fax to my editor saying, "I'm going to add a character like this!" Her design came together really quickly.

The instructor of our protagonist brothers

主人公兄弟の師匠

「精神を鍛えるには
まず「肉体から」様

どこそで 主婦を やっております。

30〜40歳代

She's from the school of "To train your spirit, first you must train your body." She's off being a housewife somewhere. 30–40 years old.

連載とかまったく考えてなかった頃の
スケッチブック らくがき。
ばけーっと色々な女の人をらくがき
してた。たぶん原型。

This is from my sketchbook, which I'd draw in when I absolutely couldn't think about the serialization. I'd just sit around, zoning out and doodling various female characters. I think this was Izumi's prototype.

イズミ師匠の設定って
スパッと決まってしまったので
初期ラフが ほとんど 無いよ。

しょうがないので
コーネロ様 初期ラフを
出すよ。

*Because I decided on Izumi's design so quickly,
I barely have any roughs of her in the early stages.
So in lieu of that, here's an early rough of Cornello.*

← 悪い顔が
ステキだよ。

His evil face is marvelous.

ABOUT THE AUTHOR

Born in Hokkaido, Japan, Hiromu Arakawa first attracted attention in 1999 with her award-winning manga *Stray Dog*. Her series *Fullmetal Alchemist* was serialized from 2001 to 2010 with a story that spanned 27 volumes and became an international critical and commercial success, receiving both the Shogakukan Manga Award and Seiun Award and selling over 70 million copies worldwide. *Fullmetal Alchemist* has been adapted into anime twice, first as *Fullmetal Alchemist* in 2003 and again as *Fullmetal Alchemist: Brotherhood* in 2009. The series has also inspired numerous films, video games and novels.

FULLMETAL EDITION
FULLMETAL ALCHEMIST
VOLUME 05

Story and Art by HIROMU ARAKAWA

Translation: AKIRA WATANABE
English Adaptation: JAKE FORBES
VIZ Media Edition Editor: JASON THOMPSON, URIAN BROWN
Touch-Up Art & Lettering: STEVE DUTRO
Design: ADAM GRANO
Editor: HOPE DONOVAN

FULLMETAL ALCHEMIST KANZENBAN vol. 5
© 2011 Hiromu Arakawa/SQUARE ENIX CO., LTD.
First published in Japan in 2011 by SQUARE ENIX CO., LTD.
English translation rights arranged with SQUARE ENIX CO., LTD. and VIZ Media, LLC.
English translation © 2019 SQUARE ENIX CO., LTD.

Printed in Canada

Published by VIZ Media, LLC
P.O. Box 77010
San Francisco, CA 94107

10 9 8 7 6 5 4
First printing, May 2019
Fourth printing, December 2023

viz.com

This is the last page.

Fullmetal Alchemist reads right to left.